W9-CHW-427

NO BORING PRACTICE, PLEASE!

FUNNY FAIRY TALE PROOFREADING

by Justin McCory Martin

NEW YORK • TORONTO • LONDON • AUCKLAND • SYDNEY
MEXICO CITY • NEW DELHI • HONG KONG • BUENOS AIRES

Teaching *Resources*

To Andrew and Colleen Martin,
my brother and his wife, newlyweds.
May you live happily ever after.

Cover design by Brian LaRossa
Cover and interior illustrations by Mike Moran
Interior design by Sydney Wright

ISBN-13: 978-0-439-58847-8
ISBN-10: 0-439-58847-2
Copyright © 2006 by Justin McCory Martin
Published by Scholastic Inc.
All rights reserved.
Printed in the U.S.A.

2 3 4 5 6 7 8 9 10   40   14 13 12 11 10 09 08 07

Contents

Mixed Review

Introduction

Proofreading are a vital skill. (This opening sentence—featuring *are* where *is* should be—probably jumped right out at you.) Of course, it's critical for students to develop a similarly sharp eye for misspellings and grammatical errors. Proofreading (removing typos, cleaning up poor punctuation) makes it possible to polish a piece of writing to a fine shine. If students can become proficient at proofreading, they will certainly become more skilled and confident as writers.

This book is designed to make it easy to learn the basics of proofreading. It features familiar fairy tale characters, such as Cinderella and Rapunzel, thrown into funny and fractured new situations. For example, there's an exercise that requires students to proofread wacky New Year's resolutions made by Goldilocks and Pinocchio. In another, students will proofread a list of new television shows such as *Sleeping Beauty Goes Undercover*.

Students will enjoy the wide variety of formats in this book, including fractured fairy tales, e-mail messages, directions, diary entries, speeches, advertisements, and even a poem. These diverse activities will keep students interested and engaged as they sharpen their proofreading skills.

The book is divided into four sections to give students practice in honing different skills. The first section is spelling, followed by punctuation and capitalization, then grammar, and finally a section on all the skills together. The progression allows students to start with the skills they are probably most familiar with and work toward the most challenging exercises in the last section. Happy proofreading to you and your students . . . from Rapunzel, Cinderella, the Big Bad Wolf, and the rest of the gang!

How to Use This Book

There are a variety of effective ways to use this book. You can reproduce the pages and have students work on them individually. You can also do the exercises together as a class. Another option: Assign students to work with partners or in teams.

The activities in this book can be used in conjunction with and as a complement to your classroom instruction. They're a great way to provide extra reinforcement for students who need more practice or review before a quiz or test. They are designed for flexible use and can be used as classwork or instant homework. At the end of the book, you'll find an answer key.

The book is organized into four sections: spelling, punctuation and capitalization, grammar, and mixed review. Follow up a mini-lesson on a writing skill with an activity that gives students practice with that skill. Once students have completed a few activities in each of the first three sections, begin to assign them the activities in the mixed skills section.

Connections to the Standards

The activities in this book are designed to support you in meeting the following writing standards outlined by Mid-continent Research for Education and Learning (McREL), an organization that collects and synthesizes national and state standards.

Uses the general skills and strategies of the writing process.
- Editing and publishing: Uses strategies to edit and publish written work (e.g., edits for grammar, punctuation, capitalization, and spelling at a developmentally appropriate level).

Uses grammatical and mechanical conventions in written compositions.
- Uses pronouns in written compositions (e.g., substitutes pronouns for nouns, uses pronoun agreement).
- Uses nouns in written compositions (e.g., uses plural and singular naming words, forms regular and irregular plurals of nouns, uses common and proper nouns, uses nouns as subjects).
- Uses verbs in written compositions (e.g., uses past and present verb tenses and verbs that agree with the subject).

- Uses conventions of spelling in written compositions (e.g., spells high-frequency, commonly misspelled words from appropriate grade-level list; uses a dictionary and other resources to spell words; uses contractions, compounds, roots, suffixes, prefixes, and syllable constructions to spell words).
- Uses conventions of capitalization in written compositions (e.g., titles of people; proper nouns; first word of direct quotations; heading, salutation, and closing of a letter).
- Uses conventions of punctuation in written compositions (e.g., uses periods after imperative sentences and in initials, and titles before names; uses commas in dates and addresses and after greetings and closings in a letter; uses apostrophes in contractions and possessive nouns; uses quotation marks around titles and with direct quotations).

Source: *Content Knowledge: A Compendium of Standards and Benchmarks for K–12 Education* (4th ed.). Mid-continent Research for Education and Learning, 2004.

Spelling

This section is devoted exclusively to spelling errors. Some spelling errors are of the "typo" variety while others are commonly misspelled words and misused homophones.

Punctuation and Capitalization

The activities in this section cover typical punctuation and capitalization errors. Punctuation skills include appropriate ending marks, comma usage, quotation marks, apostrophes in contractions and to show possession, and more. Capitalization skills include capitalizing proper nouns and first words in sentences. Students will also be on the lookout for words that are capitalized that should be lowercase.

Grammar

This section gives students practice looking for a variety of grammatical errors, such as incorrect verb tense and subject-verb agreement, as well as double negatives and other errors. Students may benefit from reading aloud the text and listening for phrases that sound incorrect.

Mixed Review

The activities in this section require students to proofread for everything: spelling, capitalization, punctuation, and grammatical errors. This is the longest section of the book because this is the kind of proofreading students will be doing on their own written work.

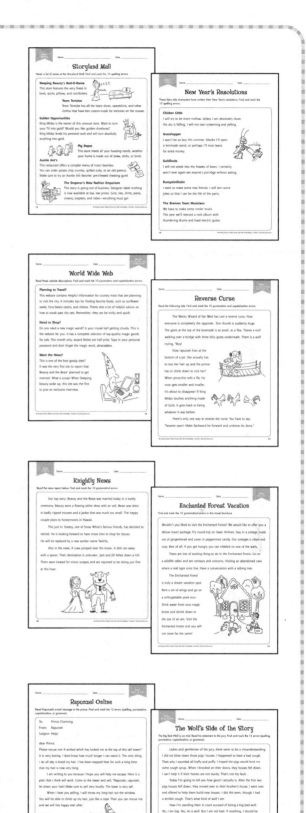

Introducing Proofreading Symbols

On page 9 there's a reproducible of common proofreading symbols. Make a copy of this page for each student, and ask students to store it in an easy-to-find location, such as in the front of their writing folders. Explain to students that these symbols are used universally so that any student, teacher, writer, editor, or anyone else who takes a pen to paper can communicate what needs to be fixed in a piece of writing. Teach a few symbols at a time in conjunction with mini-lessons on writing skills—for example, introduce the insert symbol while you are teaching students about using commas in a sequence.

Using the Answer Key

Answers for all the activities are provided at the back of the book. You might enlarge these pages on a photocopier and have students check their own work. Check that students have corrected errors properly and used the appropriate proofreading symbols to mark the text. Students may find different solutions to correct an error. For example, when there is a problem with subject-verb agreement, they could correct the verb tense or perhaps change the subject in a way that makes sense in the text. The answer key provides one possible correction for each error, but there are certainly multiple ways to edit a text.

Proofreading Symbols

Someone ~~really~~ ate my porridge.   𝓎 Delete (remove it)

certainly
Someone ~~really~~ ate my porridge.   —— Delete a word and change
to something else

             o
Someone ate my porridge.   / Delete a letter or letters and
change to something else

ate
Someone my porridge.   ∧ Insert a letter, word, or words

(lc) Someone Ate my porridge.   (lc) / Lowercase a capital letter

(cap) someone ate my porridge.   (cap) ≡ Capitalize a lowercase letter

Hey someone ate my porridge.   ⸲ Insert a comma

Someones eaten my porridge.   ˇ Insert an apostrophe

"Someone ate my porridge," he said.   ˅ ˅ Insert quotation marks

Someone ate my porridge⊙   ⊙ Insert a period

Someone ate my porridge ?   ? Insert a question mark

Someone my ate porridge.   ∩ Switch around words (transpose)

Name _____   Date _____

Fairy Tale Fortune Cookies

Here are 10 fortunes for fairy tale characters. Can you guess which character should get each one? Find and mark the 10 spelling errors. Then write the fortune number beside the appropriate character.

1. You will chop down a tall beanstallk.

2. Bridges are bad luck four you. Avoid crossing them.

3. If you have trubble sleeping, check under your mattress.

4. You wil have no trouble sleeping.

5. Be carful! Don't sneak into strange houses and eat porridge.

6. Even tho you move slowly, you will win a race.

7. Don't be late! Go staight to Grandma's!

8. If you attend a ball, make sure to be hom by midnight.

9. If you tell a li, your nose will grow.

10. Next time, build your hose with bricks instead of straw.

___ Jack

___ Tortoise

___ Goldilocks

___ Three Billy Goats Gruff

___ Little Pig

___ The Princess and the Pea

___ Little Red Riding Hood

___ Cinderella

___ Sleeping Beauty

___ Pinocchio

No Boring Practice, Please! Funny Fairy Tale Proofreading Scholastic Teaching Resources

The Poem of the Pea

Read this poem about a famous princess who couldn't fall asleep. Find and mark the
10 spelling errors.

The princess lett out a sad, sad sigh.

For though her bed was stacked 19 mattresses hi,

She found she couldn't sleep.

Even if she cownted sheep,

Her bed just felt sew lumpy.

She was geting very grumpy!

So she jumped doun from her mattress stack,

And she looked for whatevr was hurting her back.

She exspected to find her long lost doll.

If she found a whole dollhouse, it wouldn't shok her at all.

But what did the princess's weary eyes see?

She was being keept awake by just one tiny pea!

No Boring Practice, Please! Funny Fairy Tale Proofreading Scholastic Teaching Resources

11

Name _____   Date _____

Storyland Mall

Here's a list of stores at the Storyland Mall. Find and mark the 10 spelling errors.

Sleeping Beauty's Bed-O-Rama

This store features the very finest in beds, qiults, pillows, and comforters.

Team Tortoise

Team Tortoise has all the latest shoes, sweatshirts, and other clothes that have ben custom-made for tortoises on the moove.

Golden Opportunities

King Midas is the owner of this unusual store. Want to turn your TV into gold? Would you like golden shoelaces? King Midas lends his personal tuch and will turn absolutly anything into gold.

Pig Depot

This store meets all your housing needs, weather your home is made out of straw, sticks, or brick.

Auntie Ant's

This restaurant offers a complet menu of insect favorites. You can order potato chip crumbs, spilled soda, or an old peenut. Make sure to try an Auntie Ant favorite: pre-chewed chewing gum!

The Emperor's New Fashion Emporium

This story is going out of business. Designer label clothing is now available at low, low prices. Suits, ties, shirts, pants, crowns, scepters, and robes—evrything must go!

No Boring Practice, Please! Funny Fairy Tale Proofreading Scholastic Teaching Resources

SKILL:
Spelling

Bumper Stickers

Here are some bumper stickers you might see in Storyland. Find and mark the 10 spelling errors.

1. Honk if you lov porridge!

2. Elect King Midas! Vote this Tusday.

3. World's besst fairy godmother

4. World's beast gremlin grandpa

5. Proud membur of the International Sorcerer's Society

6. At midnight, this carriage turns into a pumkin.

7. Babie giant on board

8. Loves to dance in glass slipers

9. Follo me. I'm the Pied Piper.

10. I brake four beanstalks.

No Boring Practice, Please! Funny Fairy Tale Proofreading Scholastic Teaching Resources

13

Name _____   Date _____

New Year's Resolutions

These fairy tale characters have written their New Year's resolutions. Find and mark the
10 spelling errors.

Chicken Little

I will try to be more mellow. Unless I am absolutely shure
the sky is falling, I will not start screeming and yelling.

Grasshopper

I won't be so lazy this summer. Maybe I'll open
a leminade stand, or perhaps I'll moe lawns
for extra money.

Goldilocks

I will not sneak into the howses of bears. I sertainly
won't ever again eat anyone's porridge without asking.

Rumpelstiltskin

I want to make some new freinds. I will lern some
jokes so that I can be the life of the party.

The Bremen Town Musicians

We have to make some cooler music.
This year we'll reecord a rock album with
thundering drums and lowd electric guitar.

No Boring Practice, Please! Funny Fairy Tale Proofreading Scholastic Teaching Resources

Failed Tales

Here's a list of fairy tales that didn't exactly catch on. Find and mark the 10 spelling errors.

1. Sleepwalking Beuaty

2. The Goose That Laid the Invisable Eggs

3. The Majic Kazoo

4. Zach and the Slipery Celery Stalk

5. Speedy the Snail Wins His Big Rase

6. The Old Woman Who Lived in the Bottel of Glue

7. The Rapper Mouse and the Rocker Mose

8. Giganetic Polka-Dotted Skipping Hood

9. Rusty, the Tin Solder

10. The Emperor's Knew Clothespin

No Boring Practice, Please! Funny Fairy Tale Proofreading Scholastic Teaching Resources

15

Name _____   Date _____

Pumpkin Carriage Safety

Read the safety instructions for your new pumpkin carriage. Find and mark the 10 spelling errors.

Congatulations! You are the owner of a brand-new pumpkin carriage! But to truly enjoy this special vehicle, you must follow safty precautions. Remember, a pumpkin carriage is not a toy.

Only clim into the carriage using the special silk ladder. Make sure to buckel your seat belt and adjust the magic talking rearview mirror. Don't forget to lock yur doors. This can be done by presing the little mushroom knobs into the down position.

Always ware a helmet made out of a walnut shell or other hard material. Drive at a safe speed, no faster than a babbbling brook. Use the official Storyland hand signals wen making turns. Most important, do not driv a pumpkin carriage after midnight.

No Boring Practice, Please! Funny Fairy Tale Proofreading Scholastic Teaching Resources

Signs, Signs, Signs

You might see these signs in Storyland. Find and mark the 10 spelling errors.

1. Bewear of dragon

2. You must be at least 12 feet tall to rid on this giant roller coaster.

3. Free bromstick parking

4. No howling during the moovie

5. Used magic wands for sal

6. Elves workng

7. Faling sky zone: Proceed with caution

8. Speed limit: 350,000 miles per our

9. Now entering the Enchanted Forrest

10. Magic beans sold hear

No Boring Practice, Please! Funny Fairy Tale Proofreading Scholastic Teaching Resources

17

Name _____   Date _____

Royal Invitation

Read the following invitation. Find and mark the 10 punctuation and capitalization errors.

You are cordially invited to the Royal Gala Ball. It begins at 8 P.m. on Saturday, october 19. Please arrive promptly Carriage parking is available.

Dress is extremely, formal. Ladies should wear gowns? Glass slippers are optional. Gentlemen are asked to attend the ball in knightwear, which consists of a suit of armor with a tie

A 14-course dinner will be served, including soup, salad, appetizer, main course, patty cakes, and blackbird pie for Dessert. Dont forget to bring a very expensive gift. The prince needs a new set of golf clubs' (hint, hint). There will be music and dancing to the sounds of Chester jester and the Throne Tones.

No Boring Practice, Please! Funny Fairy Tale Proofreading Scholastic Teaching Resources

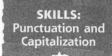

World Wide Web

Read these website descriptions. Find and mark the 10 punctuation and capitalization errors.

Planning to Travel?

This website contains Helpful information for country mice that are planning to visit the city. It includes tips for finding favorite foods, such as sunflower seeds, lima beans raisins, and cheese. Theres also a lot of helpful advice on how to sneak past city cats. Remember, they can be tricky and quick

Need to Shop?

Do you need a new magic wand? Is your crystal ball getting cloudy. This is the website for you. It has a complete selection of top-quality magic goods for sale. This month only, wizard Robes are half price. Type in your personal password and dont forget the magic word, *abracadabra*.

Want the News?

This is one of the best gossip sites?
It was the very first site to report that
Beauty and the Beast' planned to get
married. What a scoop! When Sleeping
beauty woke up, this site was the first
to post an exclusive interview.

Name _____   Date _____

Elect an Insect

The insects are electing a president. Read the candidates' speeches. Find and mark the
10 punctuation and capitalization errors.

Ant for President

I am, running for president of Fableland. The various insects that live here

need a responsible leader. Ive shown myself to be extremely responsible.

All summer, I work hard gathering seeds for the long winter. If you vote

for me, I will pass a law requiring all bugs to work very hard I will get rid of

toys televisions, and other silly distractions. Remember my slogan: "All work

and no play makes for a great day.

Grasshopper for President

Friends and fellow insects, let's have

some fun? My opponent, al Ant,

has made a number of very Boring

campaign promises. If I am elected,

I will do exactly the opposite." I will pass

a law that makes the weekend five days

long. Ill put big puddles of sticky fruit

juice at every corner of every street.

Now I'd like to introduce my running

mate, Dewey Doodlebug.

Grasshopper
for
President

Name _____ Date _____

Dear Crabby

Read the following advice column. Find and mark the 10 punctuation and capitalization errors.

Dear Crabby,

    I have a serious problem. I cant stop lying. I tell small lies, big lies, and outright whoppers. This makes gepetto very angry. He's my father, This lying gets me into all kinds of trouble.

    Worst of all, every time I tell a lie my wooden nose grows. I should also tell you that I am a distant cousin of king Tut and I often visit him in my time machine. There, I did it again! I cannot stop lying, even in this letter to you. Because I can't stop lying, my nose wont stop growing. "Please help me.

Sincerely,
Famous Wooden Puppet

Dear Famous Wooden Puppet,

    Here's my advice to you. Take up knitting This may sound strange, but it is good advice. It has worked for people with a variety of problems. Every time you have the urge to tell a fib, stop yourself and do a little knitting instead. Soon you will have a smaller Nose and some very nice sweaters

Sincerely
Crabby

Name _____   Date _____

The Little Red Hen and the Banana Split

Read the following tale. Find and mark the 10 punctuation and capitalization errors.

The Little Red Hen decided to make a delicious banana split.

She asked, "Who will go with me to the store to buy ice cream?

The dog said, "I'm Busy."

The hen asked "Who will go with me to buy whipped cream?"

The cat yawned and said, "Im not going."

The hen asked, "Who will go with me to buy bananas and cherries?"

The mule said "Count me out."

So the Little Red Hen went to the store all by herself. She bought everything necessary for a banana split: Ice cream whipped cream, bananas, and cherries. then she went home and fixed a delicious banana split.

The hen asked, "Who wants a taste?

"I do, I do," said the cat, the dog, and the mule

"Well, grab a spoon," said the Little Red Hen. "But next time, how about lending a paw or hoof to help?"

No Boring Practice, Please! Funny Fairy Tale Proofreading Scholastic Teaching Resources

Name _____   Date _____

Reverse Curse

Read the following tale. Find and mark the 10 punctuation and capitalization errors.

The Wacky Wizard of the West has cast a reverse curse. Now everyone is completely the opposite.. Tom thumb is suddenly huge. The giant at the top of the beanstalk is as small, as a flea. Theres a troll walking over a bridge with three billy goats underneath. There is a wolf crying, "Boy!

Now rapunzel lives at the bottom of a pit. She actually has to toss her hair up and the prince has to climb down to visit her? When pinocchio tells a fib, his nose gets smaller and smaller. It's about to disappear! If King Midas touches anything made of Gold, it goes back to being whatever it was before.

There's only one way to reverse the curse. You have to say: "Sesame open! Make Backward be forward and undones be done."

Name _____   Date _____

Mack the Messy Magician

Read the following tale. Find and mark the 10 punctuation and capitalization errors.

Mack was the son of the famous sorcerer merlin. When Mack was a boy, he sneaked into his dad's room in the middle of the night and found his magic Wand.

Mack pointed the wand at the carpet and said, "Abrakazoom, Abrakazi, now is the time for the carpet to fly!

Mack did not know the exact words of the spell. The carpet turned into a huge housefly that began to buzz around. Mack swung the wand at the fly and said, "Shoo"! He missed and tapped the couch with the wand. The couch turned into a giant shoe. The Shoe began to stomp loudly.

Mack didnt know what to do. He mumbled some magic words he thought he remembered his dad saying. He waved his wand Spaghetti noodles began sliding out of the walls. Mack waved the wand again. But this only caused a dancing purple goat to appear. What a mess?

Luckily, Merlin woke up. He took the wand from Mack and muttered some real magic words. Presto! everything in the castle returned to normal. Mack was grounded for 500 Years.

No Boring Practice, Please! Funny Fairy Tale Proofreading Scholastic Teaching Resources

Name _____   Date _____

Princess Team

Read the following advertisement. Find and mark the 10 punctuation and capitalization errors.

Would you like to be a member of the Storyland Princess Team. We are holding tryouts in the gym on Friday, february 28.

Youll be expected to have a routine prepared. Every routine must include a section in which you try on diamonds and other jewelry Every routine must also include some Horseback riding and archery. Remember, throughout your' tryout you must speak like a princess. Please use phrases such as "How very delightful!

We are hoping that this year's Princess Team will be the, best ever. There is room for ten girls? Please show up promptly for tryouts. Make sure to wear the proper royal outfit, including a crown cape, and very uncomfortable shoes.

Name _____ Date _____

Ogre for Hire

Read the following job application. Find and mark the 10 grammatical errors.

Your name: Otis the Ogre

Job you are applying for: Me would like to be an flight attendant on Trans Kingdom Airlines.

Why you want this job: This job would give me a chance to visit new places and eat peanuts, two of my favorite activity.

Your qualifications: I make friend very easily. I takes a bath once a year so I is very fresh smelling.

Other jobs that you have held: I use to babysit for some gnomes who lives in my neighborhood. Once I worked as a pizza delivery ogre, but that was only for one days.

Educational background: I is a graduate with honors from Ogre University.

No Boring Practice, Please! Funny Fairy Tale Proofreading Scholastic Teaching Resources

Veggie Mobiles

Cinderella traveled by pumpkin carriage to the royal ball. Here are descriptions of three other veggie mobiles. Find and mark the 10 grammatical errors.

Tomato Train

For traveling long distances, nothing beat a tomato train. The train tracks are make out of thin noodles. When you arrive at our destination, simply throw the train and tracks into a large pot. Cook for half an hour. Voilà, you have spaghetti and red sauce!

Aquatic Rescue Cabbage

This is the goodest vegetable for underwater rescue missions. Imagine that some ants was traveling in a tiny submarine that sprang a leak. You could found them quickly and save them with a aquatic rescue cabbage.

High-Speed Broccoli

Broccoli are a very boring vegetable. It usually just sits on your plate. Thanks to a spell casted by a fairy godmother, there is now a new kind of high-speed broccoli. It are perfect for space travel!

No Boring Practice, Please! Funny Fairy Tale Proofreading Scholastic Teaching Resources

27

Name _____   Date _____

Witch's Spellbook

Read these instructions for turning someone into a toad. Find and mark the
10 grammatical errors.

First, you will needs a large metal cauldron. You'll also need a long
stick for stirring. Fill the cauldron with filthy water, preferably from a bog.
Then add the following ingredient.

Toss in an raven's tail feather.
Then add the eye of a newt, which
are a very rare ingredient. If you
don't has a potion shop in your
neighborhood, simply order it
online. You should also added
a spider's web. If you can't
find one, some carpet fuzz will
works just as well. As a final touch,
sprinkle. in a few strands of
warthog hair. Stir the mixtures
with your stick.

For best results, serve the potion cold. Presto! Whoever drinks the
potion will turning into a toad. To reverse the spell, the toad must be invited
to star in an action movie. Good luck.

No Boring Practice, Please! Funny Fairy Tale Proofreading Scholastic Teaching Resources

The Queen's County Fair

Welcome to the fair! Read the descriptions of the games below. Find and mark the
10 grammatical errors.

Unicorn Ringtoss

The goal of this game
was to make a ring
land on the unicorn's
horn. Please do not
never feed peanuts
to the unicorn.

Magic Bean Count

How much magic beans are in the jar? The close guess wins a gigantic
stuffed goblin.

Dunk the Mermaid

Hit the target with a softball and the mermaid get plopped into the water
with an big splash.

Magic Carpet Rodeo

Climb aboard the bucking magic carpet. Hung on for as long as you
possibly can. The world record is just 11 second.

Greased Goblin Chase

Goblins is hard to catch, especially if them are covered in slippery oil.
Good luck!

No Boring Practice, Please! Funny Fairy Tale Proofreading Scholastic Teaching Resources

29

Name _____   Date _____

Knightly News

Read the news report below. Find and mark the 10 grammatical errors.

Our top story: Beauty and the Beast was married today in a lovely ceremony. Beauty wore a flowing white dress with an veil. Beast was dress in badly ripped trousers and a jacket that was much too small. The happy couple plans to honeymoons in Hawaii.

This just in: Sneezy, one of Snow White's famous friends, has decided to retired. He is looking forward to have more time to shop for tissues. He will be replaced by a new worker name Twitchy.

Also in the news: A cows jumped over the moon. A dish ran away with a spoon. Their destination is unknown. Jack and Jill felled down a hill. Them were treated for minor scrapes and are reported to be doing just fine at this hour.

Name _____   Date _____

Mirror, Mirror

Read the following interview with the magic mirror on the wall. Find and mark
the 10 grammatical errors.

Interviewer: Mirror, Mirror, on the wall, what are the capital of Kansas?

Mirror: Topeka.

Interviewer: Okay, we're just getting warmed up. Now I have a question
that's a little toughest. Which is heavier, a pound of feathers
or a pound of golds?

Mirror: Ooh, tricky. Their both weigh the same amount. A pound of
feathers and a pound of gold both weighing one pound.

Interviewer: Well done, Mirror. Now, I'm not going to ask you to tell I who's
the fairest of them all. You must get those question all the time.

Mirror: I do. Frankly, I'm quite bored of it.

Interviewer: Instead, I'll ask an slightly different question. Mirror, Mirror,
on the wall, who brought a ferret to the mall?

Mirror: Why, that would be Ashley Grimble.
She sneaked she's pet ferret, Fred,
into the mall in a handbag.

Interviewer: Wow, you really is good!

No Boring Practice, Please! Funny Fairy Tale Proofreading Scholastic Teaching Resources

31

Goblin Grammar

Meet Goblyn the Goblin. She has terrible grammar. Find and mark the 10 grammatical errors in her paper.

I is a smart goblin. I getted really good grades in goblin school. My favorite subject is fungus math. Here's a fungus math problem I recently solving. What do you get if you add three toadstools and two pieces of moldy cheese? Do you know the answer? You get hungry!

I am really good at sports, too. I can kick an head of rotten lettuce very far. Me am the captain of the rotten lettuce kicking team.

I'm also good behaved at home. I try to clean up my room once a week. I don't never pull on my sister's beard. Sometimes my mom serve ham and toads for dinner. That's one meal I don't like. But I always clean mine plate. In fact, I eat my plate. I am the goodest goblin in the whole wide world.

No Boring Practice, Please! Funny Fairy Tale Proofreading Scholastic Teaching Resources

Enchanted Forest Vacation

Find and mark the 10 grammatical errors in this travel brochure.

Wouldn't you liked to visit the Enchanted Forest? We would like to offer you a deluxe travel package. Fly round-trip on Swan Airlines. Stay in a cottage made out of gingerbread and cover in peppermint candy. Our cottages is clean and cozy. Best of all, if you get hungry you can nibbled on one of the walls.

There are lots of exciting thing to do in the Enchanted Forest. Go on a wildlife safari and see centaurs and unicorns. Visiting an abandoned cave where a real ogre once live. Have a conversation with a talking tree.

The Enchanted Forest is truly a dream vacation spot. Rent a set of wings and go on a unforgettable pixie tour. Drink water from ours magic brook and shrink down to the size of an ant. Visit the Enchanted Forest and you will not never be the same!

No Boring Practice, Please! Funny Fairy Tale Proofreading Scholastic Teaching Resources

33

Name _____   Date _____

New TV Shows

Read these descriptions of new TV shows. Find and mark the 12 errors (spelling, punctuation, capitalization, or grammar).

The Gingerbread Teenager

Jake is made out of gingerbread. He transfers to a new high school where all the other students are made out of Oatmeal. That's when his troubles begins. Will he make the football team Will he find a date for the annual bake sail? "If you like cookies, you will love *The Gingerbread Teenager*," rave critics.

Sleeping Beauty Goes Undercover

This is a brand-new news show. Each week Sleeping Beauty will solve a real-life crime. But here's the amazing part. Sleeping Beauty somehow manges to solve crimes without ever even waking up! Thats right. How does she do it. Tune in tuesdays at 8 to find out.

Live From Bremen Town

This is a musical show. It features the world-famous musicians from Bremen Town joined by some of his animal friends. There is a ferret playing electric guitar and an emu on the Kazoo. Other guests include iguanas beavers, and chimps. Oh my! Make sure to catch the final episode, broadcast live from the Zoo.

No Boring Practice, Please! Funny Fairy Tale Proofreading Scholastic Teaching Resources

Rapunzel Online

Read Rapunzel's e-mail message to the prince. Find and mark the 12 errors (spelling, punctuation, capitalization, or grammar).

To: Prince Charming

From: Rapunzel

Subject: Help!

dear Prince,

Pleese rescue me! A wicked which has locked me at the top of this tall tower? It is very boring. I dont know how much longer I can stand it. The only thing i do all day is braid my hair. I has been trapped hear for such a long time that my hair is now very long.

I am writing to you because I hope you will help me escape. Here is a plan that I think will work. Come to the tower and yell, "Rapunzel, rapunzel, let down your hair! Make sure to yell very loudly. The tower is very tall.

When I hear you yelling, I will throw my long hair out the window. You will be able to climb up my hair, just like a rope. Then you can rescue me and we will live happy ever after.

Sincerely

Rapunzel

No Boring Practice, Please! Funny Fairy Tale Proofreading Scholastic Teaching Resources

35

Name _____   Date _____

The Wicked Stepsister's Diary

Read the following diary entry. Find and mark the 12 errors (spelling, punctuation, capitalization, or grammar).

Dear Dairy:

I cannot believe the stunt Cinderella pulled. She was supposed to stay home last night while my sister and I went to the Third Annual royal Ball. We gave her a bunch of chores: wash, iron scrub, and sew. Instead, she showed up at the ball! Her was dressed in such fancy clothes that we didnt even recognize her.

The prince seemed very interested in cinderella. Personally, I thought she was acting silly? Right before midnight, she made a big scene about leaving in a pumpkin carriage. It was ridiculous?

Then she left behind a glass slipper. Today the prince stopped at every single house in town and begged "Try on this glass slipper." I poked in my foot, but it wasn't something Id wear in a million years. Then Cinderella tried on the slipper. It will fit her perfectly, and she made a huge deal out of it. The prince got all hyper and started saying, "I love you! I love you I love you!" Can you believe it?

Directions to Grandma's House

Read the following directions for Little Red Riding Hood to get to Grandma's. Find and mark the 12 errors (spelling, punctuation, capitalization, or grammar).

Dear Little Red Riding Hood

You should start out on the path that winds through the woods. On your left, there will be a babbling brouk. You will also pass a very tall beanstalk with a castle on top of them. Keep walking for about 1.7 miles. You will arrive at a fork in the path, right near an old oak tree. There will be two signs. One says: "To Grandma's house." The other says: "To troll bridge.

Take the path on the right. Youll pass a tall tower, and you may see a young girl named rapunzel. My word, that girl has quite a head of hair! Keep walking. I live in a little wooden cotage on the left. The address is 3217 Woods lane Terrace. You can't miss it.

One more thing, dear. Don't talk to stranger, especially wolfs. They can be very tricky. It may be a little chilly outside, so don't forget to wear your red cape? If you remember, please brings along some of those delicious cakes that your mother bakes.

Sincerely,

Grandma

No Boring Practice, Please! Funny Fairy Tale Proofreading Scholastic Teaching Resources

37

Name _____ Date _____

Dragon Den Decorating

Read the following advice for decorating a dragon's home. Find and mark the 12 errors (spelling, punctuation, capitalization, or grammar).

Dragon dens tend to be extreme gloomy places. That is probably why dragons is always in such bad moods. Here are some decorating tip to help make dragon homes more chearful.

Step one is to install some lighting. After all, caves are always, so dark. Hanging some colorfull pictures would also help.

Dragon homes get verry hot from all that fire breathing. I bet this creatures would appreciate a refrigerator stocked with cold drinks. Dragons also need a comfortible place to sit. A beanbag chair would be nice.

Clearly, one of the biggest problems for dragon's is that they are bored. They have nothing to do

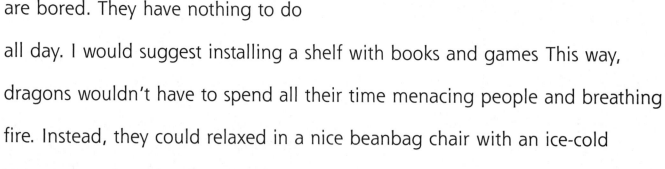

all day. I would suggest installing a shelf with books and games This way, dragons wouldn't have to spend all their time menacing people and breathing fire. Instead, they could relaxed in a nice beanbag chair with an ice-cold beverage and read a great book.

No Boring Practice, Please! Funny Fairy Tale Proofreading Scholastic Teaching Resources

Name _____   Date _____

Three Worst Wishes

Over the years the genie in the lamp has heard millions of wishes. Here are the three worst ones.
Find and mark the 12 errors (spelling, punctuation, capitalization, or grammar).

Third-Worst Wish (from Mickey Spicklesack, age 19)

"I wish that someone would invented a very small

clock that you could actually wear. That way, you

would always know the time that way. Ive seen

big clocks in houses and on towers. Wouldn't it be

cool if very small clocks existed. Personally, I think

it would make cents to wear one on your ankle."

Second-Worst Wish (from Sandy Sandals, age 38)

"I love to go to the beach. It wood be really neat to have the feeling

of being at the beach, even when I'm not there. My wish is to had sand in

my shoes for the rest of my life. That way, I would always be reminded

of the beach.

Worst Wish of All Time (from Waldo Wogwood, age 11)

"Please turn me into a superhero. Id like to be 107 foot tall and made out of

peanut butter. I would like spechal vision so that everything looks yellow to

me. Another superpower that I would like is the ability to hear grass growing.

Genie, please grant this wish".

No Boring Practice, Please! Funny Fairy Tale Proofreading Scholastic Teaching Resources

39

Name _____   Date _____

Helpful Hints for Kissing Frogs

Read the following advice. Find and mark the 12 errors (spelling, punctuation, capitalization, or grammar).

Everyone knows that if you kiss a frog, theres a chance that it will turn into a prince. Here is some helpful frog-smooching hints.

If you see a frog that is whereing a tiny crown, there is a good chance it's a prince. Frogs that wear boots or ride horses are also very promising. But be careful? These may simply be regular frogs with interesting hobbies and habits.

Talking frogs are even moore likely to be princes. Fortunately, you can simply ask them. Even if a frog can't talk, it may be able to nod it's head in response to a qeustion. You could ask: "Are you a stunningly handsum prince trapped inside a frog?

Remember, frog often move their heads in funny ways. A frog may look like it is noding in agreement. However, it may just be a regular old frog, bobbing its head up and down. then you might end up planting a big old smacker on a slimy green frog!

No Boring Practice, Please! Funny Fairy Tale Proofreading Scholastic Teaching Resources

Name _____ Date _____

One-Minute Makeovers

Read the following makeover ideas for fairy tale characters. Find and mark the 12 errors (spelling, punctuation, capitalization, or grammar).

Little Red Riding Hood

Hers red cape is very old-fashioned. She need something fresh and stylish.
She needs something that says "Look at me, everybody! I'm walking through
the woods." From now on, she will wear a really cool faded jean jacket.
Of course, she'll have to change her name to Little blue Jean Jacket.

Gingerbread Man

He is famous for saying, "You can't catch
me" But he runs everywhere barefoot. If he
isn't not careful, somebody will catch him.
Plus, he could stub one of his tows and it
might crumble right off. He desperately
needs a pair of sneakers. Maybe the
shoelaces could be make out of licorice.

Rapunzel

Her hair is a terrable mess. What do you expect if she let's it hang down
the side of a tower? She needs, a good shampoo and rinse. To keep her hair
healthy and Beautiful, it is also important that she doesn't let anyone else
climb up it.

No Boring Practice, Please! Funny Fairy Tale Proofreading Scholastic Teaching Resources

41

Name _____   Date _____

A Hare-Racing Experience

Read the following fractured tale. Find and mark the 12 errors (spelling, punctuation, capitalization, or grammar).

Everyone was excited about the big race. The hare was driving a sleek new sports Car. The tortoise was driving a minivan It was tan and needed a good washing.

On your mark, get set, go," said the announcer. The hair simply sat at the starting line revving his big, powerful engine. He got out of her car and stood in front of it so fans could take pictures.

The tortoise drove around the track very slowyl. He kept his seat belt fastened and his crash helmet in place. At one point he spotted an oil slick on the road. He drove around it very cautious and continued on his way.

suddenly, the hare realized that the tortoise had a huge head start. He hopped into his sports car and took off with a screech. Soon he was going 280 miles per hour and didn't even see the oil slick. His sports car skidded and one of the wheel's popped off. When the car finally come to a stop, the hare hopped out. His car was ruined, but luckily he wasn't hurt. Meanwhile, the tortoise drived his minivan slow across the finish line.

No Boring Practice, Please! Funny Fairy Tale Proofreading Scholastic Teaching Resources

Name _____   Date _____

Wanted by the FBI (Fairy Tale Bureau of Investigation)

Read the following sign. Find and mark the 12 errors (spelling, punctuation, capitalization, or grammar).

WANTED

Have you seen the Big Bad Wolf. He is wanted for ruining the homes of two pigs. He also attempted to destroy the home of a third pig. Witnesses overheard him saying "I'll huff and I'll puff and I'll blow your house down."

The Big bad Wolf is now number two on the most-wanted list behind the Wicked Witch. He may be traveling under a fake name, such as Rover or tinkerbell. He is very clever. Sometimes hes even known to wear a little sweater and pretending he is a poodle. Don't be fooled. Poodles do not have yellow eyes. Poodles do not have sharp Fangs, and they do not howl at the moon.

If the Big Bad Wolf nocks on your door, do not let him in. Call the Fairy Tale bureau of Investigation immediately There is a reward for any information that leads to the arrest of this creminal. The reward are five gold coins and a magic talking apple.

Name _____   Date _____

Ye New Products

Read the following advertisements for new products. Find and mark the 12 errors (spelling, punctuation, capitalization, or grammar).

Sparkle-O

You may be the fairest in the land. But who will no if your magic mirror is so dirty that you can't even see yourself. Now theres new Sparkle-O with a special magic mirror formula. It works really good.

Ogre Away

Nothing ruins a picnic like having ogres show up. They likes to make rude comments, eat your sandwiches, and spill your Juice. Fortunately, ogres hate the smel of lemon. Spray a little lemon-fresh Ogre Away at your next picnic, and these pests will stay in the bog where they belongs.

Can of Crumbs

What would you do if you was lost in the Enchanted Forest? Leaving a trail of bread crumbs is a good idea. But what if you dont have any bread? With new Can of Crumbs, you'll never have that problem again. Carry it with you everywere. Hansel and Gretel said, "We wish we had Can of Crumbs when we got lost in the woods.

Off the Wall

Read the following fractured tale. Find and mark the 12 errors (spelling, punctuation, capitalization, or grammar).

Humpty Dumpty sat on a wall. Humpty dumpty took a great fall. He land on a magic. carpet. High into the sky he flew, until he was right besides a cow that was jumping over the moon. The cow invited Humpty Dumpty to be his guessed at a royal ball that evening.

At the ball, Humpty Dumpty danced with cinderella until he grew very sleepy? He climed up a nearby beanstalk and took a nap. He slept for 20 long years.

When Humpty awoke, there was a small bear standing over him "Theres an egg sleeping in my bed! squealed the bear.

Humpty was so frightened that he ran out of the house, jumped into a pumpkin carriage, and sped through the forest. He drove and drove until he is finally home.

Name _____   Date _____

The Wolf's Side of the Story

The Big Bad Wolf is on trial. Read his statement to the jury. Find and mark the 12 errors (spelling, punctuation, capitalization, or grammar).

Ladies and gentleman of the jury, there seem to be a misunderstanding. I did not blow down those pigs' houses. I happened to have a bad cough. Thats why I sounded all huffy and puffy. I hoped the pigs would lend me some cough syrup. When I knocked on their doors, they houses fell down. I can't help it if their homes are not sturdy. That's not my fault.

Today I'm going to tell you how good I actually is. After the first two pigs houses fell down, they moved over to their bruther's house. I went over and offered to help them build new houses. I did this even, though I had a terrible cough. That's what kind of wolf I am

Now I'm standing Here in court accused of being a big bad wolf. Yes, I am big. Yes, Im a wolf. But I am not bad. If anything, I should be knowed as a big good wolf. Thank you for hering my side of the story.

No Boring Practice, Please! Funny Fairy Tale Proofreading Scholastic Teaching Resources

Name _____   Date _____

Origami Troll

Read the following directions. Find and mark the 12 errors (spelling, punctuation, capitalization, or grammar).

Origami is a japanese art form that involves folding paper into interesting and pleasing shapes. For example, you can fold paper into the shape of a swan or you can creat a paper tiger,

Today we is going to make an origami troll. First, take a clean sheet of paper and make it dirty You can scribble on it, or you might even want to step on it, leaving footprints. Good! Then, fold your's piece of paper carefully in half. Fold It one more time. You should now have a neat little sqaure.

Next, wad the paper up into a ball. Does it look like a troll. If not, wad the paper a little bite more. You might try squinting at the paper or looking at them out of the corner of your eye. You see it now, right? Congratulations, youve made an origami troll.

Size XXXXXL

Read the following passage. Find and mark the 12 errors (spelling, punctuation, capitalization, or grammar).

One of the bigest problems for giants is finding clothes that fit.
Most things are much to small. Shorts, for example, is a small piece of
clothing. But giants need really huge shorts. Sometime a giant will make
a pair of shorts out of an old tent.

In winter when it's cold, giants have trouble finding Scarves that are
big enough. Sometimes they use a long, flowing curtain. You might even
seen a giant wearing two sleeping bags for mittens.

Shoes are also always a
problem? Even the largest sizes
are too small for, giants. Often
they make their shoes out of
rowboats. Thats why giants
make such a racket when they is
walking around. This are fortunate
for peeple. If there were sneakers
for giants, you might not be able
to hear them coming!

Name _____   Date _____

Home, Sweet Castle

Read the following advertisement. Find and mark the 12 errors (spelling, punctuation, capitalization, or grammar).

For Sale

Looking for a great home? I am selling my castle, which has been in my fambily for 550 years. It has 188 room, including a tall tower with an amazing view. The drawbridge is in excellent condition. The moat has been recently clean and is freshly stocked with crocodiles.

These castle has a very large dungeon. It is dark and damp, as a good dungeon should be. There is no Electricity, so you will not be able to watch television. But you can enjoy reading by torchlight. There is also a magic harp a coat of armor that walks around, and a singing chandelier.

Bring your lawn mower! The castles yard is large, about the size of the state of maine. The castle is surrounded by an enchanted forest with elves and wood gnomes.

I'm sad to leave my huge, happy home. Im moving to the suburbs to be closer to stores. But if you is looking for a grate home in a distant kingdom, this castle might be just right. I would like to be paid in diamonds, but 10 million gold pieces would also been fine.

Name _____   Date _____

Dragon Obedience School

Read the following advertisement. Find and mark the 12 errors (spelling, punctuation, capitalization, or grammar).

Does your pet dragon behave Badly? When you leave him at home, does he rip up the couch with his claws. Does him blow smoke out of his nose and make everything dirty? If so, you may need our dragon obedience school

Does your dragon chase after airplans? Does he dig large cave in your backyard? We can teach him to obey simple commands, such as stop flying, heel roll over, and dont breathe fire.

We can also teech your dragon tricks. we can train a dragon to fetch a telephone pole or balance a refrigerator on his snout. There's nothing more cuter than watching a cuddly dragon beg for a treat. Call today for an free appointment.

No Boring Practice, Please! Funny Fairy Tale Proofreading Scholastic Teaching Resources

Sorcery School Homework

Read the following assignment. Find and mark the 12 errors (spelling, punctuation, capitalization, or grammar).

To: Second- and third-grade sorcerers

From: Mrs. Raspidoodle

You're assignment this week is to travel backward in time. Go back as far in history as you will like. You can visit America in 1776, or the Middle Ages, or ancient greece, or even go back, to cave-dwelling times.

While you are on your trip, take careful Notes. Write down everything you see, and describe the people you meets. You will be expected to write an essays about your adventure.

I need everyone to return to the pressent time by this Friday. Please dont be tardy. Also, I will ask that you do not attempt's to travel into the future. You aren't experienced enough yet to go forward in time? That's something you will learned when you are fourth-grade sorcerers.

No Boring Practice, Please! Funny Fairy Tale Proofreading Scholastic Teaching Resources

51

Name _____   Date _____

Fairy Tale Olympics

Read this newspaper article covering the Fairy Tale Olympics. Find and mark the 12 errors (spelling, punctuation, capitalization, or grammar).

This year was the greater Fairy Tale Olympics ever. The Gingerbread Man set a new records for the 100-meter dash. The Big Bad Wolf blue down seven houses in one minute, also setting a new record. Perhaps the most exciting event was pole vaulting. Pinocchio amazed the crowd by using his nose to jump over the bar?

As always, there was some controversies. King midas received a bronze medal in the troll toss and a silver medal in beanstalk climbing. Him was later spotted with two gold medals around his neck. "I didnt cheat. When I touched my medals, they turned to gold" King Midas insisted.

There was one new event that was not an success. Figure skating for mermaids is prbably not a good idea. The mermaids mostly flopped around on the ice. For the next Fairy Tale Olympics, it might be Exciting to introduce moat diving as a new event.

Favorite Storyland Bands

Check out these new bands in Storyland. Find and mark the 12 errors (spelling, punctuation, capitalization, or grammar).

Gretel The little girl who getted lost in the woods is now a teenage singing sensation. Everyone knows her biggest hit song, "I'll Leave You a Trail of Bread Crumbs, Baby".

The Backwoods Elves This is a very talented boy band. They can sing dance, and play instruments. They even makes their own shoes.

Rumpelstiltsdawg He raps about real life in Storyland. His rhymes are lightning fast and him tells great stories. His duet with Little Red riding Hood was a hug hit.

Country Mouse He wears an little cowboy hat. He plays a tiny guitar. But who isnt moved by his big voice filled with loneliness and heartbreak. When he sings, even cats start crying.

The Sword and the Stone You can call they heavy metal. You can call them hard rock. They are simply loud. Lead singer Arthur King is backed up by a 1,000-piece band that includes knights, dragons, princesses, and sorcerers,

No Boring Practice, Please! Funny Fairy Tale Proofreading · Scholastic Teaching Resources

53

Answer Key Spelling

Fairy Tale Fortune Cookies, page 10

1. You will chop down a tall beanstalk. [k]

2. Bridges are bad luck ~~four~~ for you. Avoid crossing them.

3. If you have ~~trubble~~ *trouble* sleeping, check under your mattress.

4. You wil[l] have no trouble sleeping.

5. Be car[e]ful! Don't sneak into strange houses and eat porridge.

6. Even ~~tho~~ *though* you move slowly, you will win a race.

7. Don't be late! Go st[r]aight to Grandma's!

8. If you attend a ball, make sure to be hom[e] by midnight.

9. If you tell a l[i]e, your nose will grow.

10. Next time, build your ho[u]se with bricks instead of straw.

1 Jack	**3** The Princess and the Pea
6 Tortoise	**7** Little Red Riding Hood
5 Goldilocks	**8** Cinderella
2 Three Billy Goats Gruff	**4** Sleeping Beauty
10 Little Pig	**9** Pinocchio

The Poem of the Pea, page 11

The princess let[t] out a sad, sad sigh.

For though her bed was stacked 19 mattresses ~~hi~~ *high*,

She found she couldn't sleep.

Even if she co[u]nted sheep,

Her bed just felt ~~sew~~ *so* lumpy.

She was ge[t]ting very grumpy!

So she jumped do[w]n from her mattress stack,

And she looked for whate[v]er was hurting her back.

She expected to find her long lost doll.

If she found a whole dollhouse, it wouldn't sho[c]k her at all.

But what did the princess's weary eyes see?

She was being ke[p]t awake by just one tiny pea!

Storyland Mall, page 12

Sleeping Beauty's Bed-O-Rama

This store features the very finest in beds, q[u]ilts, pillows, and comforters.

Team Tortoise

Team Tortoise has all the latest shoes, sweatshirts, and other clothes that have be[e]n custom-made for tortoises on the mo[o]ve.

Golden Opportunities

King Midas is the owner of this unusual store. Want to turn your TV into gold? Would you like golden shoelaces? King Midas lends his personal t[o]uch and will turn absolut[e]ly anything into gold.

Pig Depot

This store meets all your housing needs, ~~weather~~ *whether* your home is made out of straw, sticks, or brick.

Auntie Ant's

This restaurant offers a complet[e] menu of insect favorites. You can order potato chip crumbs, spilled soda, or an old pe[a]nut. Make sure to try an Auntie Ant favorite: pre-chewed chewing gum!

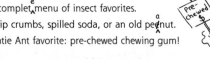

The Emperor's New Fashion Emporium

This stor[e] is going out of business. Designer label clothing is now available at low, low prices. Suits, ties, shirts, pants, crowns, scepters, and robes—ev[e]rything must go!

Bumper Stickers, page 13

1. Honk if you lov[e] porridge!

2. Elect King Midas! Vote this Tu[e]sday.

3. World's bes[t] fairy godmother

4. World's bes[t] gremlin grandpa

5. Proud memb[e]r of the International Sorcerer's Society

6. At midnight, this carriage turns into a pum[p]kin.

7. Bab[y] giant on board

8. Loves to dance in glass sli[p]pers

9. Follo[w] me. I'm the Pied Piper.

10. I brake fo[u]r beanstalks.

Answer Key Spelling

New Year's Resolutions, page 14

Chicken Little

I will try to be more mellow. Unless I am absolutely s~~h~~ure the sky is falling, I will not start scre~~e~~ming and yelling.

Grasshopper

I won't be so lazy this summer. Maybe I'll open a lem~~o~~nade stand, or perhaps I'll mo~~w~~ lawns for extra money.

Goldilocks

I will not sneak into the ho~~u~~ses of bears. I ~~c~~ertainly won't ever again eat anyone's porridge without asking.

Rumpelstiltskin

I want to make some new fr~~ie~~nds. I will le~~a~~rn some jokes so that I can be the life of the party.

The Bremen Town Musicians

We have to make some cooler music. This year we'll re~~c~~ord a rock album with thundering drums and lo~~u~~d electric guitar.

Failed Tales, page 15

1. Sleepwalking Be~~au~~ty
2. The Goose That Laid the Invis~~i~~ble Eggs
3. The Ma~~g~~ic Kazoo
4. Zach and the Sli~~p~~ery Celery Stalk
5. Speedy the Snail Wins His Big Ra~~c~~e
6. The Old Woman Who Lived in the Bott~~a~~l of Glue
7. The Rapper Mouse and the Rocker Mo~~u~~se
8. Giga~~n~~tic Polka-Dotted Skipping Hood
9. Rusty, the Tin Sold~~i~~er
10. The Emperor's ~~K~~new Clothespin (cap)

Pumpkin Carriage Safety, page 16

Cong~~r~~atulations! You are the owner of a brand-new pumpkin carriage! But to truly enjoy this special vehicle, you must follow saf~~e~~ty precautions. Remember, a pumpkin carriage is not a toy.

Only clim~~b~~ into the carriage using the special silk ladder. Make sure to buck~~al~~ your seat belt and adjust the magic talking rearview mirror. Don't forget to lock y~~o~~ur doors. This can be done by pre~~s~~sing the little mushroom knobs into the down position.

Always ~~wear~~ ware a helmet made out of a walnut shell or other hard material. Drive at a safe speed, no faster than a ba~~b~~bbling brook. Use the official Storyland hand signals w~~h~~en making turns. Most important, do not driv~~e~~ a pumpkin carriage after midnight.

Signs, Signs, Signs, page 17

1. **Beware** ~~Bewear~~ of dragon
2. You must be at least 12 feet tall to rid~~e~~ on this giant roller coaster.
3. Free bro~~o~~mstick parking
4. No howling during the mo~~o~~vie
5. Used magic wands for sal~~e~~
6. Elves work~~i~~ng
7. Fa~~l~~ling sky zone: Proceed with caution
8. Speed limit: 350,000 miles per ~~h~~our
9. Now entering the Enchanted For~~e~~st
10. Magic beans sold **here** ~~hear~~

Answer Key Punctuation and Capitalization

Royal Invitation, page 18

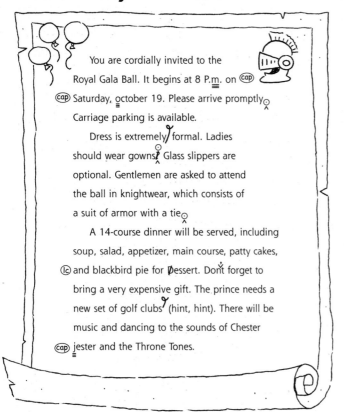

You are cordially invited to the
Royal Gala Ball. It begins at 8 P.m. on (cap)
(cap) Saturday, october 19. Please arrive promptly.
Carriage parking is available.

Dress is extremely formal. Ladies
should wear gowns. Glass slippers are
optional. Gentlemen are asked to attend
the ball in knightwear, which consists of
a suit of armor with a tie.

A 14-course dinner will be served, including
soup, salad, appetizer, main course, patty cakes,
(lc) and blackbird pie for Dessert. Don't forget to
bring a very expensive gift. The prince needs a
new set of golf clubs (hint, hint). There will be
music and dancing to the sounds of Chester
(cap) jester and the Throne Tones.

World Wide Web, page 19

Planning to Travel?

(lc) This website contains Helpful information for country mice that are planning to visit the city. It includes tips for finding favorite foods, such as sunflower seeds, lima beans, raisins, and cheese. There's also a lot of helpful advice on how to sneak past city cats. Remember, they can be tricky and quick.

Need to Shop?

Do you need a new magic wand? Is your crystal ball getting cloudy? This is the website for you. It has a complete selection of top-quality magic goods for sale. This month only, wizard Robes are half price. Type in your personal (lc) password and don't forget the magic word, *abracadabra*.

Want the News?

This is one of the best gossip sites.
It was the very first site to report that
Beauty and the Beast planned to get
married. What a scoop! When Sleeping
(cap) beauty woke up, this site was the first
to post an exclusive interview.

Elect an Insect, page 20

Ant for President

I am running for president of Fableland. The various insects that live here need a responsible leader. I've shown myself to be extremely responsible. All summer, I work hard gathering seeds for the long winter. If you vote for me, I will pass a law requiring all bugs to work very hard. I will get rid of toys, televisions, and other silly distractions. Remember my slogan: "All work and no play makes for a great day."

Grasshopper for President

Friends and fellow insects, let's have some fun! My opponent, al Ant, (cap) has made a number of very Boring (lc) campaign promises. If I am elected, I will do exactly the opposite. I will pass a law that makes the weekend five days long. I'll put big puddles of sticky fruit juice at every corner of every street. Now I'd like to introduce my running mate, Dewey Doodlebug.

Grasshopper for President

Dear Crabby, page 21

Dear Crabby,

I have a serious problem. I can't stop lying. I tell small lies, big lies, (cap) and outright whoppers. This makes gepetto very angry. He's my father. This lying gets me into all kinds of trouble.

Worst of all, every time I tell a lie my wooden nose grows. I should also tell you that I am a distant cousin of king Tut and I often visit him in (cap) my time machine. There, I did it again! I cannot stop lying, even in this letter to you. Because I can't stop lying, my nose won't stop growing. Please help me.

Sincerely,
Famous Wooden Puppet

Dear Famous Wooden Puppet,

Here's my advice to you. Take up knitting. This may sound strange, but it is good advice. It has worked for people with a variety of problems. Every time you have the urge to tell a fib, stop yourself and do a little knitting instead. Soon you will have a smaller Nose and some very (lc) nice sweaters.

Sincerely,
Crabby

Answer Key Punctuation and Capitalization

The Little Red Hen and the Banana Split, page 22

The Little Red Hen decided to make a delicious banana split. She asked, "Who will go with me to the store to buy ice cream?"

The dog said, "I'm busy." (lc)

The hen asked, "Who will go with me to buy whipped cream?"

The cat yawned and said, "I'm not going."

The hen asked, "Who will go with me to buy bananas and cherries?"

The mule said, "Count me out."

So the Little Red Hen went to the store all by herself. She bought everything necessary for a banana split: Ice cream, whipped cream, bananas, (lc) (cap) and cherries. then she went home and fixed a delicious banana split.

The hen asked, "Who wants a taste?"

"I do, I do," said the cat, the dog, and the mule.

"Well, grab a spoon," said the Little Red Hen. "But next time, how about lending a paw or hoof to help?"

Reverse Curse, page 23

The Wacky Wizard of the West has cast a reverse curse. Now everyone is completely the opposite. Tom thumb is suddenly huge. (cap) The giant at the top of the beanstalk is as small as a flea. There's a troll walking over a bridge with three billy goats underneath. There is a wolf crying, "Boy!"

(cap) Now rapunzel lives at the bottom of a pit. She actually has to toss her hair up and the prince has to climb down to visit her.

(cap) When pinocchio tells a fib, his nose gets smaller and smaller. It's about to disappear! If King Midas touches anything made (lc) of gold, it goes back to being whatever it was before.

There's only one way to reverse the curse. You have to say: (lc) "Sesame open! Make backward be forward and undones be done."

Mack the Messy Magician, page 24

Mack was the son of the famous sorcerer merlin. When Mack was a (cap) boy, he sneaked into his dad's room in the middle of the night and found his (lc) magic wand.

Mack pointed the wand at the carpet and said, "Abrakazoom, Abrakazi, now is the time for the carpet to fly!"

Mack did not know the exact words of the spell. The carpet turned into a huge housefly that began to buzz around. Mack swung the wand at the fly and said, "Shoo! He missed and tapped the couch with the wand. The couch turned into a giant shoe. (lc) The shoe began to stomp loudly.

Mack didn't know what to do. He mumbled some magic words he thought he remembered his dad saying. He waved his wand. Spaghetti noodles began sliding out of the walls. Mack waved the wand again. But this only caused a dancing purple goat to appear. What a mess!

Luckily, Merlin woke up. He took the wand from Mack and muttered some real magic words. Presto! everything in the castle returned to normal. (cap) Mack was grounded for 500 years. (lc)

Princess Team, page 25

Would you like to be a member of the Storyland Princess Team? We are holding tryouts in the gym on Friday, february 28. (cap)

You'll be expected to have a routine prepared. Every routine must include a section in which you try on diamonds and other jewelry. Every routine must also include some horseback riding and archery. Remember, (lc) throughout your tryout you must speak like a princess. Please use phrases such as "How very delightful!"

We are hoping that this year's Princess Team will be the best ever. There is room for ten girls. Please show up promptly for tryouts. Make sure to wear the proper royal outfit, including a crown, cape, and very uncomfortable shoes.

Answer Key **Grammar**

Ogre for Hire, page 26

Your name: Otis the Ogre

Job you are applying for: ~~Me~~ [I] would like to be a[n] flight attendant on Trans Kingdom Airlines.

Why you want this job: This job would give me a chance to visit new places and eat peanuts, two of my favorite activit[ies].

Your qualifications: I make friend[s] very easily. I take[s] a bath once a year so I ~~is~~ [am] very fresh smelling.

Other jobs that you have held: I use[d] to babysit for some gnomes who live[s] in my neighborhood. Once I worked as a pizza delivery ogre, but that was only for one day[s].

Educational background: I ~~is~~ [am] a graduate with honors from Ogre University.

Veggie Mobiles, page 27

Tomato Train

For traveling long distances, nothing beat[s] a tomato train. The train tracks are ma[k]e out of thin noodles. When you arrive at [y]our destination, simply throw the train and tracks into a large pot. Cook for half an hour. Voilà, you have spaghetti and red sauce!

Aquatic Rescue Cabbage

This is the ~~goodest~~ [best] vegetable for underwater rescue missions. Imagine that some ants ~~was~~ [were] traveling in a tiny submarine that sprang a leak. You could ~~found~~ [find] them quickly and save them with a[n] aquatic rescue cabbage.

High-Speed Broccoli

Broccoli ~~are~~ [is] a very boring vegetable. It usually just sits on your plate. Thanks to a spell cast[ed] by a fairy godmother, there is now a new kind of high-speed broccoli. It ~~are~~ [is] perfect for space travel!

Witch's Spellbook, page 28

First, you will need[s] a large metal cauldron. You'll also need a long stick for stirring. Fill the cauldron with filthy water, preferably from a bog. Then add the following ingredient[s].

Toss in a[n] raven's tail feather. Then add the eye of a newt, which ~~are~~ [is] a very rare ingredient. If you don't ~~has~~ [have] a potion shop in your neighborhood, simply order it online. You should also add[ed] a spider's web. If you can't find one, some carpet fuzz will work[s] just as well. As a final touch, sprinkle[/] in a few strands of warthog hair. Stir the mixture[s] with your stick.

For best results, serve the potion cold. Presto! Whoever drinks the potion will turn[ing] into a toad. To reverse the spell, the toad must be invited to star in an action movie. Good luck.

The Queen's County Fair, page 29

Unicorn Ringtoss

The goal of this game ~~was~~ [is] to make a ring land on the unicorn's horn. Please do not [n]ever feed peanuts to the unicorn.

Magic Bean Count

How ~~much~~ [many] magic beans are in the jar? The close[st] guess wins a gigantic stuffed goblin.

Dunk the Mermaid

Hit the target with a softball and the mermaid get[s] plopped into the water with a[n] big splash.

Magic Carpet Rodeo

Climb aboard the bucking magic carpet. H[a]ng on for as long as you possibly can. The world record is just 11 second[s].

Greased Goblin Chase

Goblins ~~is~~ [are] hard to catch, especially if the[y] are covered in slippery oil. Good luck!

Answer Key Grammar

Knightly News, page 30

Our top story: Beauty and the Beast ~~was~~ _were_ married today in a lovely ceremony. Beauty wore a flowing white dress with a_n_ veil. Beast was dress_ed_ in badly ripped trousers and a jacket that was much too small. The happy couple plans to honeymoon_s_ in Hawaii.

This just in: Sneezy, one of Snow White's famous friends, has decided to retire_d_. He is looking forward to hav_ing_ more time to shop for tissues. He will be replaced by a new worker name_d_ Twitchy.

Also in the news: A cow_s_ jumped over the moon. A dish ran away with a spoon. Their destination is unknown. Jack and Jill fell~~ed~~ down a hill. The_y_m were treated for minor scrapes and are reported to be doing just fine at this hour.

Mirror, Mirror, page 31

Interviewer: Mirror, Mirror, on the wall, what ~~are~~ _is_ the capital of Kansas?

Mirror: Topeka.

Interviewer: Okay, we're just getting warmed up. Now I have a question that's a little toughe_r_. Which is heavier, a pound of feathers or a pound of gold_?_

Mirror: Ooh, tricky. The_y_ both weigh the same amount. A pound of feathers and a pound of gold both weighi_ng_ one pound.

Interviewer: Well done, Mirror. Now, I'm not going to ask you to tell + _me_ who's the fairest of them all. You must get ~~those~~ _that_ question all the time.

Mirror: I do. Frankly, I'm quite bored of it.

Interviewer: Instead, I'll ask a_n_ slightly different question. Mirror, Mirror, on the wall, who brought a ferret to the mall?

Mirror: Why, that would be Ashley Grimble. She sneaked ~~she's~~ _her_ pet ferret, Fred, into the mall in a handbag.

Interviewer: Wow, you really ~~is~~ _are_ good!

Goblin Grammar, page 32

I ~~is~~ _am_ a smart goblin. I gett~~ed~~ really good grades in goblin school. My favorite subject is fungus math. Here's a fungus math problem I recently solvi~~ng~~ _ed_. What do you get if you add three toadstools and two pieces of moldy cheese? Do you know the answer? You get hungry!

I am really good at sports, too. I can kick a_n_ head of rotten lettuce very far. ~~Me~~ _I_ am the captain of the rotten lettuce kicking team.

I'm also ~~good~~ _well_ behaved at home. I try to clean up my room once a week. I don't _n_ever pull on my sister's beard. Sometimes my mom serve_s_ ham and toads for dinner. That's one meal I don't like. But I always clean ~~mine~~ _my_ plate. In fact, I eat my plate. I am the ~~goodest~~ _best_ goblin in the whole wide world.

Enchanted Forest Vacation, page 33

Wouldn't you like~~d~~ to visit the Enchanted Forest? We would like to offer you a deluxe travel package. Fly round-trip on Swan Airlines. Stay in a cottage made out of gingerbread and cover_ed_ in peppermint candy. Our cottages ~~is~~ _are_ clean and cozy. Best of all, if you get hungry you can nibble~~d~~ on one of the walls.

There are lots of exciting thing_s_ to do in the Enchanted Forest. Go on a wildlife safari and see centaurs and unicorns. Visit~~ing~~ an abandoned cave where a real ogre once live_d_. Have a conversation with a talking tree.

The Enchanted Forest is truly a dream vacation spot. Rent a set of wings and go on a_n_ unforgettable pixie tour. Drink water from our_s_ magic brook and shrink down to the size of an ant. Visit the Enchanted Forest and you will ~~not~~ never be the same!

Answer Key Mixed Review

New TV Shows, page 34

The Gingerbread Teenager

Jake is made out of gingerbread. He transfers to a new high school where all the other students (lc)are made out of Oatmeal. That's when his troubles begins. Will he make the football team? Will he find a date for the annual bake ~~sale~~(sale)? "If you like cookies, you will love *The Gingerbread Teenager*," rave critics.

Sleeping Beauty Goes Undercover

This is a brand-new news show. Each week Sleeping Beauty will solve a real-life crime. But here's the amazing part. Sleeping Beauty somehow manges(a) to solve crimes without ever even waking up! That's right. How does she do it? Tune in tuesdays at 8 to find out. (cap)

Live From Bremen Town

This is a musical show. It features the world-famous musicians from Bremen Town joined by some of ~~his~~(their) animal friends. There is a ferret playing electric guitar and an emu on the Kazoo. Other guests include iguanas, beavers, (lc) and chimps. Oh my! Make sure to catch the final episode, broadcast live from (lc)the Zoo.

Rapunzel Online, page 35

To: Prince Charming
From: Rapunzel
Subject: Help!

(cap)dear Prince,

Please rescue me! A wicked ~~which~~(witch) has locked me at the top of this tall tower! It is very boring. I dont know how much longer I can stand it. The only thing (cap)i do all day is braid my hair. I ~~has~~(have) been trapped ~~hear~~(here) for such a long time that my hair is now very long.

I am writing to you because I hope you will help me escape. Here is a plan that I think will work. Come to the tower and yell, "Rapunzel, rapunzel,(cap) let down your hair! Make sure to yell very loudly. The tower is very tall.

When I hear you yelling, I will throw my long hair out the window. You will be able to climb up my hair, just like a rope. Then you can rescue me and we will live ~~happy~~(happily) ever after.

Sincerely,
Rapunzel

The Wicked Stepsister's Diary, page 36

Dear Diary:

I cannot believe the stunt Cinderella pulled. She was supposed to stay home last night while my sister and I went to the Third Annual royal Ball. (cap) We gave her a bunch of chores: wash, iron, scrub, and sew. Instead, she showed up at the ball! ~~Her~~(She) was dressed in such fancy clothes that we didnt even recognize her.

The prince seemed very (cap)interested in cinderella. Personally, I thought she was acting silly. Right before midnight, she made a big scene about leaving in a pumpkin carriage. It was ridiculous!

Then she left behind a glass slipper. Today the prince stopped at every single house in town and begged, "Try on this glass slipper." I poked in my foot, but it wasn't something Id wear in a million years. Then Cinderella tried on the slipper. It ~~will~~ fit her perfectly, and she made a huge deal out of it. The prince got all hyper and started saying, "I love you! I love you! I love you!" Can you believe it?

Directions to Grandma's House, page 37

Dear Little Red Riding Hood,

You should start out on the path that winds through the woods. On your left, there will be a babbling brook. You will also pass a very tall beanstalk with a castle on top of ~~them~~(it). Keep walking for about 1.7 miles. You will arrive at a fork in the path, right near an old oak tree. There will be two signs. One says: "To Grandma's house." The other says: "To troll bridge."

Take the path on the right. Youll pass a tall tower, and (cap) you may see a young girl named rapunzel. My word, that girl has quite a head of hair! Keep walking. I live in a little wooden cotage on the left. The address is 3217 Woods lane Terrace.(cap) You can't miss it.

One more thing, dear. Don't talk to strangers especially ~~wolfs~~(wolves). They can be very tricky. It may be a little chilly outside, so don't forget to wear your red cape. If you remember, please bring along some of those delicious cakes that your mother bakes.

Sincerely,
Grandma

Answer Key Mixed Review

Dragon Den Decorating, page 38

Dragon dens tend to be extreme~ly~ gloomy places. That is probably
why dragons ~is~ (are) always in such bad moods. Here are some decorating tip~s~ to
help make dragon homes more che~e~rful.

Step one is to install some lighting. After all, caves are always' so dark.
Hanging some colorful' pictures would also help.

Dragon homes get very' hot from all that fire
breathing. I bet ~this~ (those) creatures would appreciate
a refrigerator stocked with cold drinks.
Dragons also need a comfort~a~ble place to sit.
A beanbag chair would be nice.

Clearly, one of the biggest
problems for dragon's is that they
are bored. They have nothing to do
all day. I would suggest installing a shelf with books and games⊙ This way,
dragons wouldn't have to spend all their time menacing people and breathing
fire. Instead, they could relax~ed~ in a nice beanbag chair with an ice-cold
beverage and read a great book.

Three Worst Wishes, page 39

Third-Worst Wish (from Mickey Spicklesack, age 19)
"I wish that someone would invent~ed~ a very small
clock that you could actually wear. That way, you
would always know the time ~that way~. I've seen
big clocks in houses and on towers. Wouldn't it be
cool if very small clocks existed? Personally, I think
it would make ~cents~ (sense) to wear one on your ankle."

Second-Worst Wish (from Sandy Sandals, age 38)
"I love to go to the beach. It ~wood~ (would) be really neat to have the feeling
of being at the beach, even when I'm not there. My wish is to ha~ve~ sand in
my shoes for the rest of my life. That way, I would always be reminded
of the beach."

Worst Wish of All Time (from Waldo Wogwood, age 11)
"Please turn me into a superhero. I'd like to be 107 ~foot~ (feet) tall and made out of
peanut butter. I would like spec~i~al vision so that everything looks yellow to
me. Another superpower that I would like is the ability to hear grass growing.
Genie, please grant this wish!"

Helpful Hints for Kissing Frogs, page 40

Everyone knows that if you kiss a frog, there's a chance that it will turn
into a prince. Here ~is~ (are) some helpful frog-smooching hints.

If you see a frog that is ~whereing~ (wearing) a tiny crown, there is a good chance
it's a prince. Frogs that wear boots or ride horses are also very promising.
But be careful! These may simply be regular frogs with interesting hobbies
and habits.

Talking frogs are even more' likely to be princes. Fortunately, you can
simply ask them. Even if a frog can't talk, it may be able to nod it's head in
response to a q~u~estion. You could ask: "Are you a stunningly hands~ome~ prince
trapped inside a frog?"

Remember, frog~s~ often
move their heads in funny
ways. A frog may look like it is
no~d~ding in agreement. However,
it may just be a regular old
frog, bobbing its head up and
(cap) down. then you might end up
planting a big old smacker
on a slimy green frog!

One-Minute Makeovers, page 41

Little Red Riding Hood
Her' red cape is very old-fashioned. She need~s~ something fresh and stylish.
She needs something that says, "Look at me, everybody! I'm walking through
the woods." From now on, she will wear a really cool faded jean jacket.
Of course, she'll have to change her name to Little blue Jean Jacket. (cap)

Gingerbread Man
He is famous for saying, "You can't catch
me!" But he runs everywhere barefoot. If he
isn't ~not~ careful, somebody will catch him.
Plus, he could stub one of his to~e~s and it
might crumble right off. He desperately
needs a pair of sneakers. Maybe the
shoelaces could be ma~d~e out of licorice.

Rapunzel
Her hair is a terr~i~ble mess. What do you expect if she let's it hang down
the side of a tower? She needs' a good shampoo and rinse. To keep her hair
(lc) healthy and beautiful, it is also important that she doesn't let anyone else
climb up it.

Answer Key Mixed Review

A Hare-Racing Experience, page 42

Everyone was excited about the big race. The hare was driving a sleek (lc)new sports ¢ar. The tortoise was driving a minivan⌐It was tan and needed a good washing.

ˇOn your mark, get set, go," said the announcer. The ~~hair~~^hare simply sat at the starting line revving his big, powerful engine. He got out of ~~her~~^his car and stood in front of it so fans could take pictures.

The tortoise drove around the track very slow⌐ly. He kept his seat belt fastened and his crash helmet in place. At one point he spotted an oil slick on the road. He drove around it very cautious^ly and continued on his way.

(cap) suddenly, the hare realized that the tortoise had a huge head start. He hopped into his sports car and took off with a screech. Soon he was going 280 miles per hour and didn't even see the oil slick. His sports car skidded and one of the wheel's popped off. When the car finally c^ame to a stop, the hare hopped out. His car was ruined, but luckily he wasn't hurt. Meanwhile, the tortoise ~~drived~~^drove his minivan slow^ly across the finish line.

Wanted by the FBI (Fairy Tale Bureau of Investigation), page 43

WANTED

Have you seen the Big Bad Wolf? He is wanted for ruining the homes of two pigs. He also attempted to destroy the home of a third pig. Witnesses overheard him saying^"I'll huff and I'll puff and I'll blow your house down."

(cap) The Big bad Wolf is now number two on the most-wanted list behind the Wicked Witch. He may be traveling under a fake name, such as Rover or tinkerbell. (cap) He is very clever. Sometimes he's even known to wear a little sweater and pretend~~ing~~he is a poodle. Don't be fooled. Poodles do not have yellow eyes. Poodles (lc)do not have sharp ƒangs, and they do not howl at the moon.

If the Big Bad Wolf^knocks on your door, do not let him in. Call the (cap) Fairy Tale bureau of Investigation immediately⌐There is a reward for any information that leads to the arrest of this cr^iminal. The reward ~~are~~^is five gold coins and a magic talking apple.

Ye New Products, page 44

Sparkle-O

You may be the fairest in the land. But who will ~~no~~^know if your magic mirror is so dirty that you can't even see yourself? Now there's new Sparkle-O with a special magic mirror formula. It works really ~~good~~^well.

Ogre Away

Nothing ruins a picnic like having ogres show up. They like's to make rude comments, eat your sandwiches, and spill your ʃuice. Fortunately, ogres hate (lc) the smel^l of lemon. Spray a little lemon-fresh Ogre Away at your next picnic, and these pests will stay in the bog where they belongʃ.

Can of Crumbs

What would you do if you ~~was~~^were lost in the Enchanted Forest? Leaving a trail of bread crumbs is a good idea. But what if you don't have any bread? With new Can of Crumbs, you'll never have that problem again. Carry it with you every^where. Hansel and Gretel said, "We wish we had Can of Crumbs when we got lost in the woods."ˇ

Off the Wall, page 45

Humpty Dumpty sat on (cap) a wall. Humpty dumpty took a great fall. He land^ed on a magic ʃcarpet. High into the sky he flew, until he was right beside ʃa cow that was jumping over the moon. The cow invited Humpty Dumpty to be his ~~guessed~~^guest at a royal ball that evening.

At the ball, Humpty Dumpty danced with ḏinderella until he grew (cap) very sleepy⌐He climbed up a nearby beanstalk and took a nap. He slept for 20 long years.

When Humpty awoke, there was a small bear standing over him⌐ "There's an egg sleeping in my bed!ˇ squealed the bear.

Humpty was so frightened that he ran out of the house, jumped into a pumpkin carriage, and sped through the forest. He drove and drove until he ~~is~~^was finally home.

Answer Key Mixed Review

The Wolf's Side of the Story, page 46

Ladies and gentleman of the jury, there seem[s] to be a misunderstanding. I did not blow down those pigs' houses. I happened to have a bad cough. Thats why I sounded all huffy and puffy. I hoped the pigs would lend me some cough syrup. When I knocked on their doors, ~~they~~ [their] houses fell down. I can't help it if their homes are not sturdy. That's not my fault.

Today I'm going to tell you how good I actually is [am]. After the first two pigs' houses fell down, they moved over to their br[o]ther's house. I went over and offered to help them build new houses. I did this even though I had a terrible cough. That's what kind of wolf I am.

Now I'm standing [h]ere in court accused of being a big bad wolf. Yes, I am big. Yes, i'm a wolf. But I am not bad. If anything, I should be know[n]ed as a big good wolf. Thank you for h[a]ering my side of the story.

Origami Troll, page 47

Origami is a [J]apanese art form that involves folding paper into interesting and pleasing shapes. For example, you can fold paper into the shape of a swan or you can creat[e] a paper tiger.

Today we is [are] going to make an origami troll. First, take a clean sheet of paper and make it dirty. You can scribble on it, or you might even want to step on it, leaving footprints. Good! Then, fold your[s] piece of paper carefully in half. Fold [i]t one more time. You should now have a neat little sq[u]are.

Next, wad the paper up into a ball. Does it look like a troll? If not, wad the paper a little bit[e] more. You might try squinting at the paper or looking at ~~them~~ [it] out of the corner of your eye. You see it now, right? Congratulations, youv'e made an origami troll.

Size XXXXXL, page 48

One of the big[g]est problems for giants is finding clothes that fit. Most things are much to[o] small. Shorts, for example, is [are] a small piece of clothing. But giants need really huge shorts. Sometime[s] a giant will make a pair of shorts out of an old tent.

In winter when it's cold, giants have trouble finding [s]carves that are [lc] big enough. Sometimes they use a long, flowing curtain. You might even see[n] a giant wearing two sleeping bags for mittens.

Shoes are also always a problem. Even the largest sizes are too small for giants. Often they make their shoes out of rowboats. Thats why giants make such a racket when they is [are] walking around. This are [is] fortunate for pe[o]ple. If there were sneakers for giants, you might not be able to hear them coming!

Home, Sweet Castle, page 49

For Sale

Looking for a great home? I am selling my castle, which has been in my fam[i]ly for 550 years. It has 188 room[s], including a tall tower with an amazing view. The drawbridge is in excellent condition. The moat has been recently clean[ed] and is freshly stocked with crocodiles.

~~These~~ [This] castle has a very large dungeon. It is dark and damp, as a good dungeon should be. There is no [e]lectricity, so you will not be able to watch television. But you can enjoy reading by torchlight. There is also a magic harp, a coat of armor that walks around, and a singing chandelier.

Bring your lawn mower! The castle's yard is large, about the size of the state of [M]aine. The castle is surrounded by an enchanted forest with elves and wood gnomes.

I'm sad to leave my huge, happy home. Im moving to the suburbs to be closer to stores. But if you is [are] looking for a ~~grate~~ [great] home in a distant kingdom, this castle might be just right. I would like to be paid in diamonds, but 10 million gold pieces would also be[en] fine.

Answer Key Mixed Review

Dragon Obedience School, page 50

(lc)   Does your pet dragon behave ̶B̶adly? When you leave him at home, does he rip up the couch with his claws? Does ~~him~~ᵸᵉ blow smoke out of his nose and make everything dirty? If so, you may need our dragon obedience school.

Does your dragon chase after airplan̶s̶ᵉ? Does he dig large cave̶s̶ in your backyard? We can teach him to obey simple commands, such as stop flying, heel, roll over, and don't breathe fire.

We can also te̶a̶ch your (cap)dragon tricks. ̲we̲ can train a dragon to fetch a telephone pole or balance a refrigerator on his snout. There's nothing ~~more~~ cuter than watching a cuddly dragon beg for a treat. Call today for a̶n̶ free appointment.

Sorcery School Homework, page 51

To: Second- and third-grade sorcerers
From: Mrs. Raspidoodle

~~You're~~ Your assignment this week is to travel backward in time. Go back as far in history as you ~~will~~ would like. You can visit America in 1776, or the Middle (cap)Ages, or ancient greece, or even go back to cave-dwelling times.

While you are on your trip, take careful ̶N̶otes. Write down everything (lc) you see, and describe the people you meet̶s̶. You will be expected to write an essay̶s̶ about your adventure.

I need everyone to return to the present time by this Friday. Please don't be tardy. Also, I will ask that you do not attempt̶'̶s̶ to travel into the future. You aren't experienced enough yet to go forward in time. That's something you will learn̶e̶d̶ when you are fourth-grade sorcerers.

Fairy Tale Olympics, page 52

This year was the great̶er̶ᵉˢᵗ Fairy Tale Olympics ever. The Gingerbread Man set a new record̶s̶ for the 100-meter dash. The Big Bad Wolf ~~blue~~ blew down seven houses in one minute, also setting a new record. Perhaps the most exciting event was pole vaulting. Pinocchio amazed the crowd by using his nose to jump over the bar̶.̶!

As always, there ~~was~~ were some controversies. King ̲midas̲ received a bronze (cap) medal in the troll toss and a silver medal in beanstalk climbing. ~~Him~~ᴴᵉ was later spotted with two gold medals around his neck. "I didn't cheat. When I touched my medals, they turned to gold," King Midas insisted.

There was one new event that was not a̶n̶ success. Figure skating for mermaids is pr̶o̶bably not a good idea. The mermaids mostly flopped around on the ice. For the next Fairy Tale Olympics, it might be ̶E̶xciting to introduce (lc) moat diving as a new event.

Favorite Storyland Bands, page 53

Gretel The little girl who ~~getted~~ got lost in the woods is now a teenage singing sensation. Everyone knows her biggest hit song, "I'll Leave You a Trail of Bread Crumbs, Baby.̶"̶

The Backwoods Elves This is a very talented boy band. They can sing, dance, and play instruments. They even make̶s̶ their own shoes.

Rumpelstiltsdawg He raps about real life in Storyland. His rhymes are lightning fast and ~~him~~ᵸᵉ tells great stories. His duet with Little Red ̲riding Hood̲(cap) was a hug̶e̶ hit.

Country Mouse He wears a̶n̶ little cowboy hat. He plays a tiny guitar. But who isn't moved by his big voice filled with loneliness and heartbreak? When he sings, even cats start crying.

The Sword and the Stone You can call ~~they~~ them heavy metal. You can call them hard rock. They are simply loud. Lead singer Arthur King is backed up by a 1,000-piece band that includes knights, dragons, princesses, and sorcerers.